D0250908

LOW BUDGET TRICKS
FOR SMALL SPACES

smart investing
@ your library®

A partnership between American Library Association
and FINRA Investor Education Foundation

ALA American Library Association

FINRA Investor Education FOUNDATION

FINRA is proud to support the American Library Association

WITHDRAWN

LOW BUDGET TRICKS
FOR SMALL SPACES

MONTSE BORRÀS, EDITOR

FIREFLY BOOKS

A FIREFLY BOOK

Published by Firefly Books Ltd. 2013

Copyright © 2013 LOFT Publications

All rights reserved. No part of this publication
may be reproduced, stored in a retrieval system,
or transmitted in any form or by any means,
electronic, mechanical, photocopying, recording or
otherwise, without the prior written permission of
the Publisher.

First printing

Publisher Cataloging-in-Publication Data (U.S.)

A CIP record for this title is available from the
Library of Congress

**Library and Archives Canada Cataloguing in
Publication**

A CIP record for this title is available from Library
and Archives Canada

Published in the United States by
Firefly Books (U.S.) Inc.
P.O. Box 1338, Ellicott Station
Buffalo, New York 14205

Published in Canada by
Firefly Books Ltd.
50 Staples Avenue, Unit 1
Richmond Hill, Ontario L4B 0A7

Cover design: Erin R. Holmes/Soplari Design

Printed in China

LOFT Publications, S.L.
Via Laietana, 32, 4°, of. 92
08003 Barcelona, Spain

For Loft:
Editor: Claudia Martínez Alonso
Editorial assistant: Ana Marques
Art direction:Mireia Casanovas Soley
Layout:Laia Pampalona Expósito

© Eugeni Pons

If you don't feel comfortable in your home and need to redecorate a space, or if you would simply like to give your home a new look and think that your budget is not big enough, the following pages contain 200 ideas that will provide you with inspiration for redecorating the interior of your home and for expressing your personality in your surroundings. By following these simple tips and playing with materials, colors, styles, accessories, lighting and other components, you can transform your home without having to spend a great deal of money.

Carrying out a low-cost decorating project requires strategic planning, and, of course, time and patience. Some of the things you should consider before embarking on a project of this kind are: requesting quotes from different suppliers and shops, comparing prices to decide which features you can make savings on, recycling furniture and using leftover paint. Despite having to stick to a budget, the aim is to enjoy this experience without having to resort to hiring a professional. To help you achieve this, the book is structured around the main spaces of a house: kitchens, bathrooms, bedrooms, home offices, living rooms and passageways.

Whatever environment you wish to decorate, there are a few basic rules that apply to any space. It is always best to keep areas clear, with just a few well-chosen decorative features. There is no need to invest in new features: you could renovate any vintage piece, taking advantage of the fact that vintage is in vogue right now, or reupholster a chair to give a corner a personal touch. To save money, you could always replace cupboards, which are among the most expensive pieces in a house, with curtains and rails, making use of an opening in a wall or creating one with a partition wall.

Another fundamental element is color; this can totally transform the look of a space with minimal investment. Minimalist-style neutral tones help to create harmony and give plenty of light, although you can still use a more daring color for a specific point or apply vinyl paint to separate environments within a single space.

In short, it is a question of prioritizing. It is not about wiping the slate clean, but rather eliminating superfluous features to decorate a space economically and efficiently. Most importantly, it is about converting a project into reality, while enjoying each step of the process.

© Luis Hevia

© Luis Hevia

© Peter Bennetts

© Peter Bennetts

Etched glass panels divide the little studio from the living area. When closed, they still allow light to filter through.

© Vercruysse & Dujardin / owi.bz

© Sharrin Rees

© Sharrin Rees

© Ralf Feiner

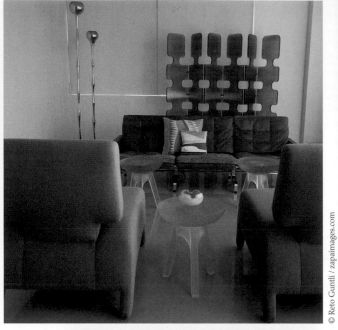

© Reto Guntli / zapaimages.com

© Reto Guntli / zapaimages.com

Decorative features and colors add a special touch to the living room.

© Reto Guntli / zapaimages.com

© Jordi Miralles

© Jordi Miralles

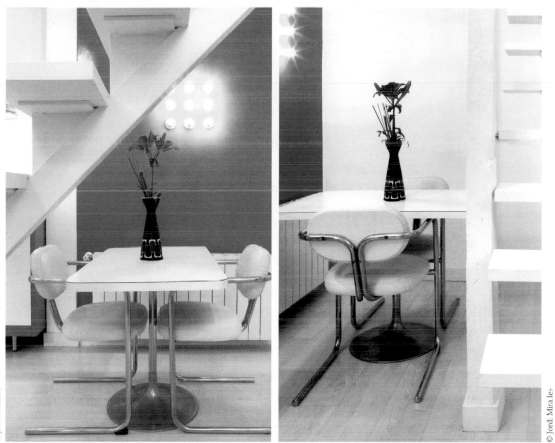

© Jordi Miralles

© Jordi Mira les

© Óscar Gutiérrez

© Óscar Gutiérrez

The living room's intimate atmosphere is the result of a combination of straight lines, some select pieces of furniture, and deep, rich colors enhanced by warm textures, such as a thick, soft woolen rug in the sitting area.

The coldness of the polished cement and aluminum structure is counteracted by the explosion of colors in the brick floor and in the built-in cupboards that stretch from wall to wall.

© Peter Bennetts

© Peter Bennetts

© Verne / owi.bz

© Matevz Paternoster

© Cover

Classic 20th-century furniture can accept any type of
pattern and help create welcoming atmospheres.

© Jordi Miralles

© Sharrn Rees

© Sharrin Rees

Shiny and glossy surfaces dominate the living room. Mirrors play an essential part, reflecting the light and increasing the feeling of spaciousness.

© Eugeni Pons

© Eugeni Pons

© Undine Pröhl

Date due: 3/28/2016,23:59
Title: Small spaces :
maximizing limited spaces for
liv
Call number: 747.1/WILHIDE

Item ID: 31336084048041
Date charged: 3/6/2016,16:48

Total checkouts for session:3

Total checkouts:4

<><><><><><><><><><><
><>
Renew at
www.sandiegolibrary.org
OR Call 619-236-5800 or
858-484-4440 and press 1
then 2 to RENEW. Your
library card is needed to
renew borrowed items.

The two spaces function as separate atmospheres inside the apartment. At varying times of the day they allow different degrees of intimacy.

© Pierrick Bourgoin

© Pierrick Bourgoin

© Pierrick Bourgoin

© Sadahiro Shimizu / Atelier A5

© Sadahiro Shimizu / Atelier A5

© Jacques Dirand

© Jacques Dirand

The dining area is raised on a wooden platform, which creates a subtle separation from the living room. The area by the main entrance is used as a casual breakfast nook.

© Jacques Dirand

© John M. Hall

© John M. Hall

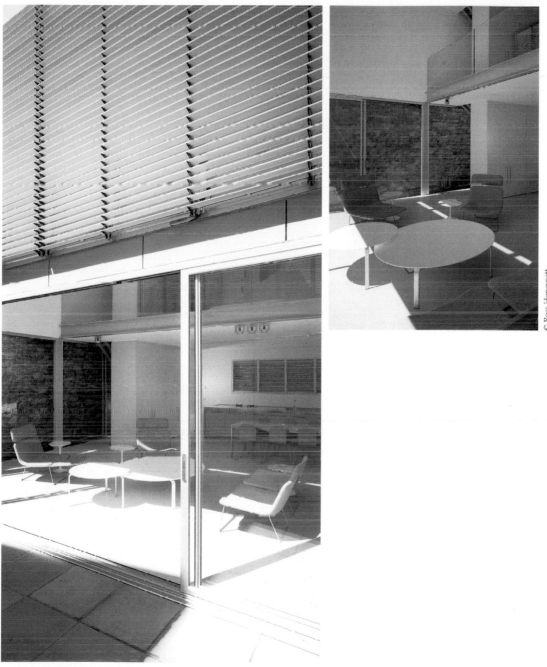

© Ross Honeysett

© Ross Honeysett

Decorative motifs are used on the various pieces
of furniture, producing unique and very personal
atmospheres. It is also possible to establish a relation
between the flooring motifs and those that embellish
the furniture by using similar patterns and colors.

© Ulf Celander

© Anima LLC Architecture & Design

© Anima LLC Architecture & Design

© Lars Hallén, Arno de la Chapelle

© Lars Hallén, Arno de la Chapelle

© Vincent Knapp

Contrasting elements from different styles and periods are framed within a duality of black and white. The thick, soft rug in the living room balances the feeling of spaciousness produced by the generous height of the ceilings.

© Esto Photography, Jeff Goldberg

© Esto Photography, Jeff Goldberg

© Esto Photography y Jeff Goldberg

© Redcover

This sheer patterned curtain with large colored dots filters the light and creates a relaxed and cheerful atmosphere. It is the perfect choice for this living room, furnished with pieces of different styles.

This apartment has the added bonus of plenty of storage space, but the open concept and well-planned lighting also help to convey a feeling of spaciousness.

© Richard Dean

© Richard Dean

© Ricardo Labougle

© Ángel Baltanás

© Ángel Baltanás

© Ángel Baltanás

© Rob 't Hart

The texture and color of the concrete roof, as well as the large panes of glass in the communal area, allow the indoor living space to integrate smoothly with its forested surroundings.

© Rob 't Hart

© Rob 't Hart

The open scheme of the living room and the fact that it has various sliding-door entrances allow the space to be accessible at any given moment.

© Virginia del Giudice

© Virginia del Giudice

The generous amount of light and the orderly layout of the apartment have made it possible for this small space to have a classical look and feel, so that all the beloved pieces can be included without losing its spacious appeal.

© Virginia del Giudice

© Virginia del Giudice

© Virginia del Giudice

© Ángel Baltanás

© Ángel Baltanás

© Sharrin Rees

© Sharrin Rees

© Sharrin Rees

© Sharrin Rees

© Paolo Utimpergher

© Paolo Utimpergher

© Bart van Leuven

© Luis Hevia

© Hiroyuki Hirai

© Hiroyuki Hirai

The windows, both in the walls and in the roof, were carefully placed to create different effects: to expand or reduce the space, to frame panoramic views, and to bring the outside indoors.

© Hiroyuki Hirai

A stone staircase leads to the home, which is on the
second floor. The right-angle extension of the second
step gives way to a bench that provides extra seating
space in the central area of the studio.

© Pep Escoda

© Pep Escoda

67

© Philippe Harden

© Philippe Harcen

Shelves stretch along the hallway, which connects the two main rooms. White walls and ceilings contrast with the gray color of the central living space.

© Cover

© Cover

© Eugeni Pons

© Sharrin Rees

© Sharrin Rees

The long, central interior is divided into two parts by
the mirrored corridor; one side houses the bathroom
and kitchen and the other side is dedicated to the
main rooms, thus creating a sense of spaciousness.

© Tom Ferguson.

© Luis Hevia

© Luis Heviz

© Eugeni Pons

© Verne / owi.bz

© Cover

In the staircase area, the same geometric pattern
reins in the progression of levels, creating a changing
effect as you go up or down the stairs.

The corridors of this home have been painted with large strips of different colors and widths, bringing to mind a barcode. The idea is to create an optical illusion around the staircase and add a playful retro look to the most neutral spaces of the home.

© Reto Guntli / zapaimages.com

© Reto Guntli / zapaimages.com

© Sharin Rees

© Sharin Rees

Combining motifs on the basis of their thematic content is an attractive and ingenious idea: decorative plates inspired by Roman art history are superimposed over wallpaper with Roman arches to create a special thematic ambiance.

© Redcover

© Luis Hevia

© Esto Photography, Jeff Goldberg

Polycarbonate has been used as a low-cost substitute for glass in this property.

© Nicholas Kane

© Sharrin Rees

© Ignacio Martínez

© Ignacio Martínez

© Gogortza & Llorella

© Eugeni Pons

© Eugeni Pons

© Esto Photography, Jeff Goldberg

© Esto Photography, Jeff Goldberg

© Eugeni Pons

© Eugeni Pons

© Eugeni Pons

© Eugeni Pons

© Eugeni Pons

© Nicholas Kane

© Tom Ferguson

© Tom Ferguson

© Pep Escoda

© Mateo Piazza

© Alberto Muciaccia

© Alberto Muciaccia

© David Cardelús

© David Cardelús

© David Cardelús

© Pep Escoda

© Pep Escoda

© Fernando Guerra

© Jordi Miralles

© John M. Hall

Every last detail of this small New York apartment has been designed and built to make the most of the light and the space.

© Karin Hessmann, Dieter Leistner / Artur

© Eugeni Pons

© Eugeni Pons

© Cannatà & Fernandes Arquitectos

© Cannatà & Fernandes Arquitectos

© Sharrin Rees

© Alvise Silenzi

© Vercruysse & Dujardin / owi.kz

© Ross Honeysett

© Mar Mottreneo

Furniture can be used to define spaces. The table is anchored to the wall to define the kitchen and dining areas.

© Peter Bennetts

© Peter Bennetts

JUICE
DIET COKE
←SARDINES

© Nicholas Kane

Expressed through furniture and interior design, this home's austere and simple themes emphasize the low-cost architectural approach.

The open kitchen serves as an island, which separates this area from the dining area, which can also be separated by a large polycarbonate sliding panel.

© Carlos Emilio

© Carlos Emilio

© Carlos Errilio

Cedar siding, that is typically seen used in exterior applications, were used on interior walls, but painted a much lighter color, to finish the surfaces.

© Torben Eskerod

© Torben Eskerod

© Redcover

Motif applications have invaded kitchens, too.
A stimulating space is achieved by combining
elements of day-to-day use with colors similar to
that of the décor.

© Ricardo Labougle

© Ricardo Labougle

This kitchen is fully integrated into the space through its system of movable panels. Due to its playful colors, it is also a very striking decorative element.

These digital prints applied directly to furniture are a perfect way to personalize a very neutral space, such as a modern kitchen. The most mundane objects become original decorative elements when enlarged and applied to the furniture.

© Ben Rahm

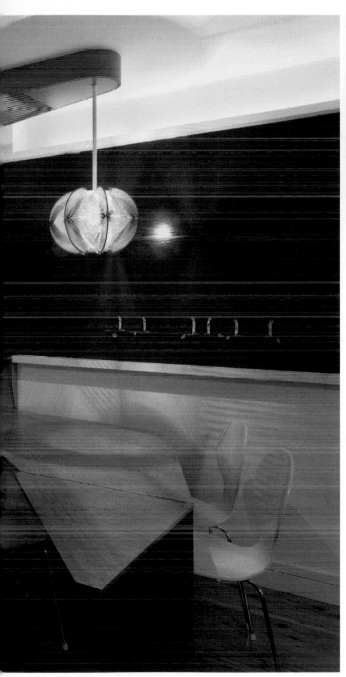

© Ben Rahn

In order to minimize the visual barriers, only a subtle change in the flooring marks the boundaries between the kitchen, living room, and courtyard.

© John M. Hall

The kitchen, the bedroom and the living room become a single space when the glass panels are tucked away. Then, the TV can be turned around to face the living room.

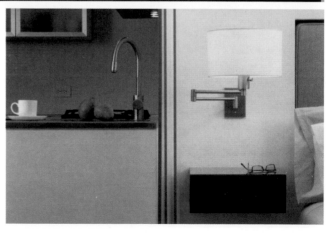

© John M. Hall

© John M. Hall

© Philippe Harden

© Philippe Harden

© Philippe Harden

© Aliocha Merker

© Aliocha Merker

Running parallel to the kitchen counter, the red PVC wall is the only chromatic element of the project. It conceals a dressing room and storage space.

Using plywood and ordinary furniture helps to keep
every detail of the building within budget.

© Karin Hessmann, Dieter Leistner / Artur

© Björn Magnea

© Björn Magnea

© Ignacio Martínez

© Ignacio Martínez

© Undine Pröhl

© Undine Pröhl

All the interior surfaces are made of plywood panels for good insulation and a rich texture.

© Reto Guntli / zapaimages.com

© Reto Guntli / zapaimages.com

Unity is achieved in this project by using the same finish across all similar surfaces; walls, floors and ceilings are painted or finished with the same materials.

© Esto Photography, Jeff Goldberg

© Esto Photography, Jeff Goldberg

© Paúl Rivera / Archphoto

© Raúl Rivera / Archphoto

© Raúl Rivera / Archphoto

© Jordi Miralles

© James Wilkins

© Óscar Gutiérrez

© Óscar Gutiérrez

© Óscar - Gutiérrez

© Tom Ferguson

© Tom Ferguson

© Tom Ferguson

Inspired by futuristic films from the '60s and '70s, this small attic's walls and furniture have rounded, organic shapes. All kitchen elements are merged into one custom-built piece of furniture.

© Vercruysse & Dujardin / owi.bz

© Vercruysse & Dujardin / owi.bz

© Verruysse & Dujardin / owi.bz

© Pierrick Bourgoin

© Pierrick Bourgoin

© María Masieri

The concrete is finished with simple manual sanding, which significantly reduces not only the cost of the project, but also the completion time.

© María Masieri

© Luis Hevia

Lively colors have been used to contrast the predominant white color and cement textures of the apartment.

© Luis Hevia

© Luis Hevia

© Pierrick Bourgoin

© Emilio Tremolada, Tiziano Sartorio, Jürgen Eheim

© Emilio Tremolada, Tiziano Sartorio, Jürgen Eheim

© Emilio Tremolada, Tiziano Sartorio, Jürgen Eheim

© Emilio Tremolada, Tiziano Sartorio, Jürgen Eheim

© Sharrin Rees

The design elements of the '70s add a distinctive style to the dining and living areas. The mirrors in the open kitchen impart a bar counter look.

© Sharrin Rees

© Eugeni Pons

© Ole Holst

© Ulf Celander

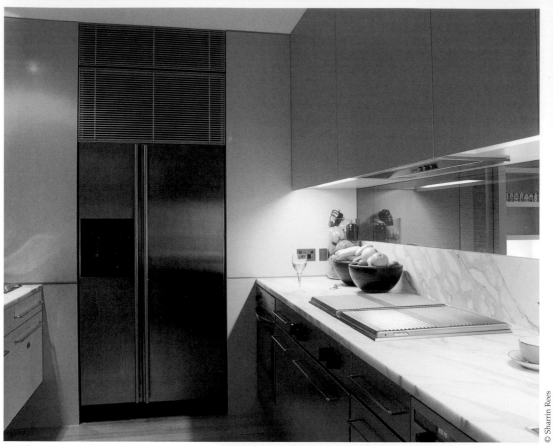

© Sharrin Rees

© Sharrin Rees

© Paolo Utimpergher

© James Wilkins

© James Wilkins

The same lines of coziness and warmth are kept in all the rooms. The bathroom and bedroom are divided by a glass brick wall that allows passage of light but separates functions, while preserving intimacy.

© Óscar Gutiérrez

© Óscar Gutiérrez

© Óscar Gutiérrez

© Ben Rahn / A-Frame

As the evening advances, sunlight filters through the openings in the façade, creating a changing pattern of light and shade inside the home.

© Ben Rahn / A-Frame

© Verne / owi.bz

Using polycarbonate allowed the creation of
uniquely designed doors and windows.

© Nicholas Kane

© Reto Guntli / zapaimages.com

© Björg Magnea

In the search for natural light, an interesting set of reflections is generated by the space itself through the different openings.

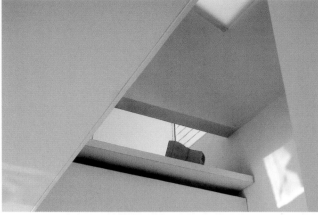

© Nicholas Kane

Nicholas Kane

© John M. Hall

© John M. Hall

© Fernandes & Capanema

© Sharrin Rees

© Sharrin Rees

© Sharrin Rees

© Pierrck Bourgoin

© Eugeni Pons

© Eugeni Pons

© Eugeni Pons

© Carlos Emilio

© Ross Honeysett

© Ross Honeysett

This house has natural cross-ventilation, thanks to large sliding windows and adjustable glass blinds.

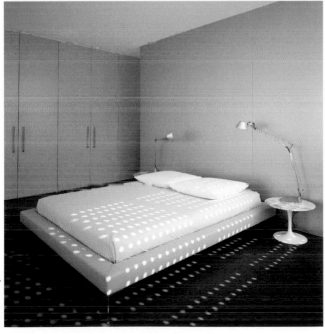

© Ross Honeysett

The sleeping area, on an upper level, enriches the interior space by creating different heights.

© Ole Holst

© Ole Holst

© Ángel Baltanás

© Ricardo Labougle

© Pierrick Bourgoin

Circles of different sizes and colors are arranged to form rays of a larger circle, producing a kaleidoscope effect.

© Torben Eskerod

© Torben Eskerod

© Jacques Dirand

© Vincent Knapp

© Bart van Leuven

© Bart van Leuven

© Stephan Zähring

A Japanese feel has been created from soft
light-blue stripes.

© Ángel Baltanás

© Ángel Baltanás

© Sharin Rees

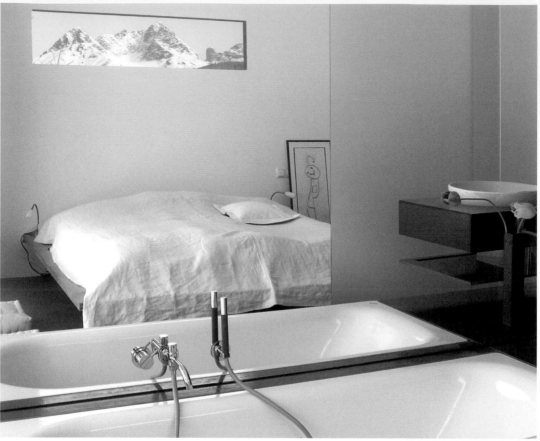

© Johannes Felsch, Caramel

© Ángel Baltanás
© Ángel Baltanás

© Björg Magnea

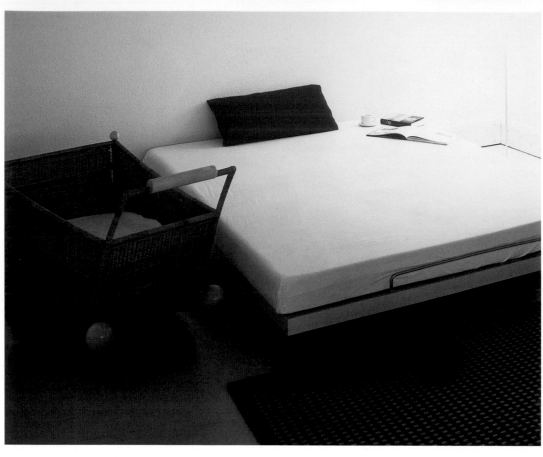

© Karin Hessmann, Dieter Leistner / Artur

© Jordi Miralles

© Marc Mormeneo

Using a minimal amount of furniture in the area designated for the bedroom avoids interference with its architectural concept: a space that captures light.

© Marc Mormeneo

© Anima LLC Architecture & Design

© Tom Ferguson

© Richard Dean

© Ben Rahn

© Sharrin Rees

© Luigi Filetici

© Luigi Filetici

© Luigi Filetici

Greater visual depth is achieved in the bathroom by means of a glass panel that separates the shower from the rest of the space.

© Luigi Filetici

© Verne / owi.bz

In this apartment, the use of mirrors in large surfaces
magnifies all the rooms, creating a genuine feeling
of spaciousness.

© Sharrin Rees

© Sharrn Rees

© James Wilkins

© James Wilkins

© Vincent Knapp

© Luis Hevia

This apartment is an open space where various islands are designed to fulfill different functions. These islands are organized around a central interior with hinged panels that conceal the bathtub and the bedroom.

© Luis Hevia

The peculiar rounded wall that surrounds the bathroom stands out on the upper floor, and its multicolored mosaic breaks up the continuity of the white.

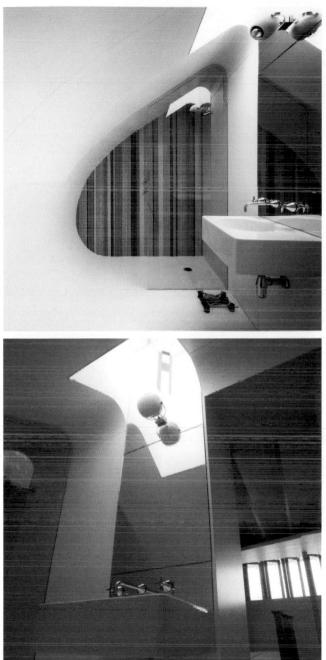

© Ben Rahn

A skylight supported by a copper chimney provides natural light and ventilation in the bathroom, and it constitutes a perfect point of reference to locate the house at night.

© Pierrick Bourgoin

© Pierrick Bourgoin

All the woodwork was custom-made using Macassar Ebony, which provides great homogeneity to the entire apartment.

© Ross Honeysett

© Luis Hevia

© Luis Heva

© Aliocha Merker

© Aliocha Merker

© Manuel Serrano Arquitectos

© Sharrin Rees

© Sharrin Rees

© Hirotaka Satoh

© Pierrick Bourgoin

Cut-out holes serve as shelving throughout the apartment and can be customized to fit other elements such as the bathroom mirror.

© Verstrysse & Dujardin / owi.bz

© Ricardo Labougle

© Ricardo Labougle

While the area with the best lighting was used for the living spaces, the most enclosed and private area was used for the storage closet and bathroom.

© Eugeni Pons

The transoms allow light in and soften the impact of
the bathroom furniture in the room.

© Ignacio Martínez

© Luis Hevia

The bathtub, with its streaked white marble surfaces and theatrical curtains, is the only luxurious element among the otherwise humble selection of materials that represent the industrial past of the apartment.

© Hiroyuki Hirai

© Anima LLC Architecture & Design

© Anima LLC Architecture & Design

© Carlos Emilio

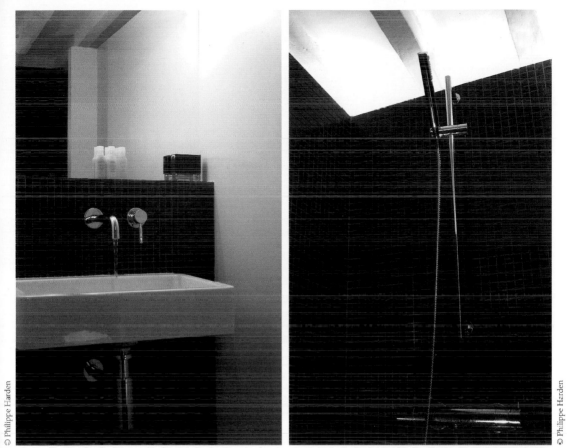

© Philippe Harden

© Philippe Harden

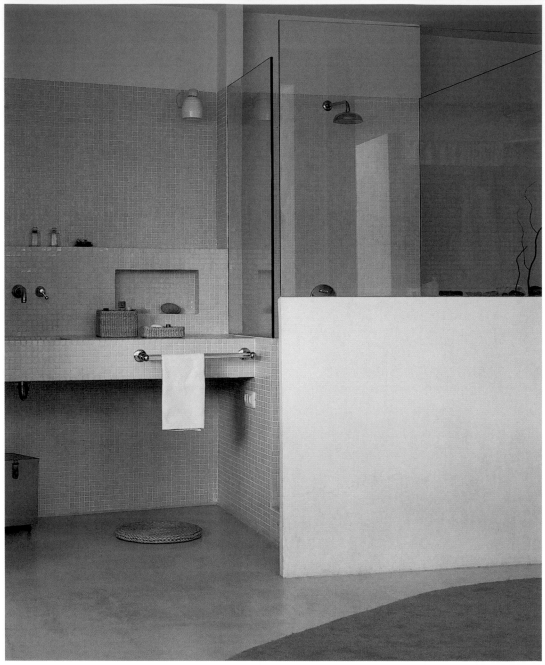

© Eugeni Pons

© Richard Dean

The bathroom walls are clad with tiles that combine different shades of green, with bright orange adding a striking touch of color.

© John M. Hall

© Jacques Dirand

© Bart van Leuven

© Undine Pröhl

© Eugeni Pons

© Eugeni Pons

© Reto Guntli / zapaimages.com

© Paúl Rivera / Archphoto

© Martina Issler, Peter Würmli

© Björg Magnea

© M3 Architects

© Marc Mormeneo